The New English Landscape

Jason Orton
Ken Worpole

The New English Landscape

Field Station | London

'We can never neatly separate what we see from what we know.'
— E. H. Gombrich, *The Story of Art*, 1950

Contents

1 Landscape as heritage

The new English landscape of this essay is an imaginative construct, a personal attempt to meld together historic, æsthetic and ecological elements around the issues of habitat, landscape and sense of place which have been in play in Britain since the end of the Second World War. Like many, I believe that a unique political settlement was achieved in 1945, changing the attitudes of people towards each other, to their life opportunities, and to a new world being created around them. This settlement elided a decline of social deference with a more outgoing attitude towards social and geographical mobility, which, with increased wealth and opportunities for holidays and outdoor recreation, democratised attitudes to the landscape and access to it.

The 1944 Greater London Plan developed pre-war proposals for 'green belts' along with linear parks linking town to country. The Town and Country Planning Act of 1947 and the National Parks and Access to the Countryside Act of 1949 regulated for a more equitable mix of work, life and leisure, the latter act being described by one proponent, Lewis Silkin, as 'a people's charter – a people's charter for the open-air'. Pressure for such policies had been building up since the highly publicised 'right to roam' and public trespass campaigns of the 1930s.

The year of 1949 also saw the setting up of the Nature Conservancy (later reorganised into separate Scottish, Welsh and English organisations), bringing together the work of a number of local and regional nature conservation societies. The Youth Hostel Association continued to recruit, with nearly 250,000 members by 1947, and in 1951 *The Country Code* was published by the National Parks Commission, a guide to town dwellers on how to treat the countryside with respect. In this unprecedented era of national reconstruction, planning, nature conservation and landscape appreciation were mutually reinforcing fields of public policy (partly because so many key people were simultaneously involved in all three). Even in the midst of war, a commitment to creating public access to the coastline was being fervently discussed, with one government planner arguing that 'we have only one coast and it is neither a local, nor even regional, but a national possession. It is the consciousness of the coast as a whole which needs quickening.' That ideal has now been largely achieved.

The 1944 Greater London Plan proposals for linear parks eventuated in the Lea Valley Regional Park, occupying a landscape well known to my family then and now: my father cycled into Epping Forest and Hertfordshire from Stratford at weekends in the 1930s, whilst my father-in-law was a member of Eton Manor Boys' Club on the Hackney Marshes. In turn, his sister's Girl Guide Brigade in Bethnal Green regularly hiked or went camping in Epping Forest and beyond, sometimes being invited for tea by their patron, Christina Foyle, at her country house near Maldon. I have the pocket diaries my mother kept in 1931 and 1932 recording almost daily outings to Victoria Park and walks along the Lea with her girlfriends, sometimes to watch the rowing, but more regularly to go to the dirt-track racing at Lea Bridge Stadium and West Ham Stadium in the evenings. For a number of years my wife and I owned a small canal boat, moored on the Lea in Hackney, spending weekends exploring the nearby canals and waterways.

Many Londoners discovered a spiritual home along the River Lea, and further out in the Essex reaches, and loyalty to this 'bastard' countryside is complex and enduring. The distinctive topography of the Lea Valley remains hallowed ground. Combining industry, agriculture, leisure and recreation, ecology and a tumultuous social history, it was a prototype of a new kind of landscape which emerged after the war, a model of how a working landscape could be seen to possess æsthetic and communitarian qualities. Such hybrid landscapes capture the ambivalent feelings we all have about our wavering loyalties between town and country, the life of the street and the solitude of the woodland walk or coastal footpath.

Not everybody accepts the validity of these landscapes, let alone their renegade æsthetics. In 2003 the magazine *Country Life* published a survey of the landscape qualities of the English counties and in doing so awarded Essex no marks at all for landscape quality. The charitable might say that *Country Life*'s assessors lacked imagination. They had failed to notice that the 20th century had been and gone, leaving considerable æsthetic confusion in its wake. Nearly a hundred years before Thomas Hardy predicted, in connection with his description of the gloomy Egdon Heath, 'that one day people would go for harsher surroundings when looking for beauty: in Iceland rather than the vineyards of southern Europe, on the beaches of Scheveningen rather than in the spa towns of Baden or Heidelberg.' Before him the painter John Constable wrote that 'I never saw an ugly thing in my life,' going on to record that 'the sound of water escaping from mill-dams, willows, old rotten planks, slimy posts, and brickwork, I love such things. These scenes made me a painter, and I am grateful.'

In short there is a crisis of representation and exposition in landscape æsthetics. Lofty statements on the true and the beautiful are increasingly resisted as the particularities and historical complexities of local and regional topographies — especially those of former industrial areas — are evaluated anew. The very notion of a defined series of 'Areas of Outstanding Natural Beauty', protected by statutory regulation, raises more questions than it answers. One remembers the sceptical words of Raymond Williams, who in *The Country and the City* observed that a working country is hardly ever described as a landscape. Today, when there is a return to the idea of more self-sufficient local and regional economies, with an interest in local produce and sustainable agriculture, it seems a good time to revisit that assumption.

These are deeply political matters. 'National identity would lose much of its ferocious enchantment without the mystique of a particular landscape tradition,' historian Simon Schama has argued, 'its topography mapped, elaborated, and enriched as a homeland.' Attachment to place, in its myriad forms, needs to be understood as constituting one of the most vital elements of landscape æsthetics.

Place and identity

In February 2006 the UK belatedly endorsed the European Landscape Convention (also known as the Florence Convention) adopted by the Council of Europe on 20 October 2000, and which came into force on 1 March 2004. Article 5 states that 'each party undertakes to recognise landscapes in law as an essential component of people's surroundings, an expression of the diversity of their shared cultural and natural heritage, and a foundation of their identity.' Directives from Europe are frequently a matter of indifference or derision, even though most advances in environmental protection now enjoyed in the UK originated in Brussels rather than being pioneered at home.

A growing appreciation of the importance of place now goes to the heart of politics, public æsthetics and cultural identity. At an advisory level, initiatives such as the *Landscape Character Assessment*, commissioned and published by the Countryside Agency (merged with English Nature to become Natural England on 1 October 2006), have been important in creating a framework for understanding the many benefits of landscape assessment and appreciation in a wider context. Yet consensus on æsthetic issues — what is valued and what is regarded as unloved and possibly unlovable — remains hard to find.

The hard and fast distinction once made between town and country is no longer tenable in many parts of Britain today, especially as road building, housing development and retail parks have extended deep into former rural terrain, whilst at the same time agriculture itself has industrialised. Concluding what was then regarded as a definitive history, *The Making of the English Landscape* (1955), W. G. Hoskins excoriated what had been done to England in the first half of the 20th century, pronouncing it beyond recuperation. 'Since the year 1914, every single change in the English landscape has either uglified it or destroyed its meaning,' Hoskins exclaimed, 'above all in eastern England.' Population growth and suburbanisation were principally to blame, he wrote, though Oliver Rackham later countered this by asserting that 'modern agriculture is by far the principal culprit for the destruction of the historic landscape.' Many other books and studies have since confirmed that government agricultural policy since the Second World War up until recently, emphasising intensive farming techniques, has resulted in a laying waste to wildlife and much distinctive landscape character.

Yet every new generation develops an attachment to the landscape close to where they live, giving the lie to the idea that all change is for the worse, and that the golden age was always in the past, or only just within living memory, now gone forever. There is today a wide and rich vocabulary employed to describe these new hybrid landscapes, ranging from the relatively benign 'suburbia' to the scathing 'drosscape'. Poets Paul Farley and Michael Symmons Roberts have written an entire book about this morphology, settling on the generic term 'edgelands'. The naturalist Richard Mabey got there first, however, with his pioneering study of the ecology of urban decay, *The Unofficial Countryside*, first published in 1973. Mabey remains the most persuasive chronicler of these strange transformations, and in his recent book, *Weeds*, explains how the old binaries of urban and rural, nature and culture, are no longer meaningful:

> The development of cultivation was perhaps the single most crucial event informing our modern notions of nature. From that point on the natural world could be divided into two conceptually different camps: those organisms contained, managed and bred for the benefit of humans, and those which are 'wild', continuing to live in their own territories on, more or less, their own terms. Weeds occur when this tidy compartmentalisation breaks down. The wild gatecrashes our civilised domains, and the domesticated escapes and runs riot. Weeds vividly demonstrate that natural life — and the course of evolution itself — refuse to be constrained by our cultural concepts. In doing so they make us look closely at the very idea of a divided creation.

While it is heartening that a rich ecology can now be seen to exist in many former industrial sites, in rural areas the loss of habitat and biodiversity remains shocking. In Essex alone, 75 percent of coastal grazing marsh has been lost since the 1930s, along with 95 percent of hay meadows with their profusion of wild flowers, as well as nearly 50 percent of ancient woodland. Of 30,000 hectares of inter-tidal salt marsh that surrounded the Essex coast 400 years ago, only 2,500 hectares remain. This loss of biodiversity is replicated throughout much of the UK.

The requirement to interpret and re-evaluate contemporary landscapes — especially those which resist traditional categories of taste — is therefore vital. A full discussion about landscape æsthetics offers a rare opportunity in which social and environmental imperatives could be reconciled in a 21st century politics of place. However, it is an arena in which there are few easy compromises. The 19th century French writer and provincial politician, Jules Reynard, wrote that, 'as a mayor, I am responsible for the upkeep of rural roads. As a poet I would prefer to see them neglected.' In earlier times the English satirist Richard Owen Cambridge said that he hoped to die and go to heaven before the then fashionable landscape designer Lancelot 'Capability' Brown arrived to 'improve it'.

A similar ambivalence afflicts many today, torn between accepting things as they are (and possibly hankering after an 'unimproved' world) and imagining things as they might be. There are good reasons why many who live close to the Lea Valley site — transformed beyond recognition for the 2012 London Olympics — had grave fears that a unique landscape, though polluted and in poor shape, yet patently rich in its industrial and cultural heritage, was in danger of being eradicated entirely. Such apprehensions were graphically expressed in the strangely melancholic drawings of artist Laura Oldfield Ford. Those anxieties have been confirmed. Though designed as if minted new, and apparently note perfect ecologically, the new Queen Elizabeth Park has entirely erased the memory of what existed there before, along a river valley whose importance as the home of the 'second industrial revolution' had incalculable historic and landscape value, equal to the Ironbridge Gorge. The Lea Valley's role in the development of aeronautics, telecommunications, chemicals and the early film industry, as well as acting as London's kitchen garden and water basin, created over time a unique landscape combining the pastoral and the industrial, and providing the subject of several volumes of detailed history by industrial historian Dr Jim Lewis, an enthusiast still in thrall to this 'bastard landscape' as many of us are.

For more than a hundred years Essex served as a laboratory for many of the major economic and land use changes which have occurred in Britain since the industrial revolution, while acting as the expansionary frontier of London, its unruly progenitor. Until the 20th century the county included all the present day local authorities of Waltham Forest, Newham, Barking & Dagenham, Redbridge and Havering. The industrial and artisan culture — along with the close-packed streetscapes of east London — once permeated into the county, though it is now in retreat or has been administratively severed, thus creating a new ambiguous terrain rapidly filling up with retail warehouses and low-rise housing. 'Essex is odd,' wrote theatre critic Michael Coveney in his biography of actor Ken Campbell, 'it's all East End overspill, yet strangely rural round the edges. It has London's heartbeat but exists as an experimental compromise between the town and the country, the expanding city and the defiant swamp-lands.'

In recent decades these economic disruptions and demographic shifts have engendered cultural and political consequences too. London's eastern estates once produced militant industrial and craft trades unionism, as well as radical social and cultural movements from within large swathes of tenement dwellings and overcrowded streets. De-industrialisation and suburbanisation (along with improved standards of living) produced other kinds of aspirations, principally for a more private, domestic lifestyle associated with home owner-ship and greater social and geographical mobility. The rise of 'Essex man', a term deployed to mythologise a former industrial militant who had become a conservative voting individualist, added to this sense that Essex was a testing ground for wider patterns of political and cultural change. The 'estuary accent' — the flat London convivial argot of the docks and the street market — was adopted as a signifier of today's 'classless' popular culture, even amongst an urban cultural elite.

Essex, East Anglia and Englishness

British topographical writing has been dominated in recent times by the landscapes of East Anglia, with an increasing interest in the particularities of estuarine Essex. If landscape and national identity are uneasy familiars or surrogates of each other, it is worth asking what is Englishness today if its favoured topography is based on the low horizons and cold seas of its eastern approaches? Why does the zeitgeist now favour a lonelier, bleaker, more rebarbative sense of place?

It cannot just be proximity to London. In the late 19th and early 20th centuries a growing number of British artists' colonies were located as far from industry, commerce and metro-politan life as was possible. Today the romance of the remote is no longer a part of landscape æsthetic. If anything, the opposite is the case. Since the Second World War there has been a growing emphasis on the vernacular and familiar as equally worthy of artistic interest, and in which Essex rural life and topography have featured prominently. Its low lying, arable landscapes — with telegraph poles, ruined barns, decoy ponds and isolated farms — along with still lively villages and market towns, are evident in the drawings by John Nash for John Pudney's 1944 collection of seasonal sonnets, *Almanack of Hope*, or in Thomas Hennell's draw-ings for C. Henry Warren's Essex diaries, *The Land is Yours*, as well as *Miles from Anywhere*, both published in 1944. Edward Bawden provided exact, luminous illustrations based on Great Bardfield life for the King Penguin *Life in an English Village* (1949) and in 1950 the eminent book illustrator, Lynton Lamb, devoted a whole book to the architecture and townscape of Chelms-ford, *County Town: Backs and Fronts in Kennelsford* (1950).

Some of this interest was triggered by the war itself. In her account of the 'Recording Britain' project — an early wartime initiative created to record valued buildings, artefacts and landscapes in case they were destroyed — historian Gill Saunders observes that 'Essex was considered to be a likely area for invasion', and artists were sent in 'before the county was occupied by the British, or the German army'. Established in the winter of 1939, this project — whose full title was 'Scheme for Recording the Changing Face of Britain' — was in effect a rallying cry for Englishness, exemplified in watercolours recording rural churches, historic country houses, village streets and cultivated landscapes. However, some examples of vernacular landscapes, nonconformist chapels and industrial streetscapes did slip through the net, including significant works featuring Essex by Walter Baynes, Hercules Du Plessis and Kenneth Rowntree.

Meanwhile Eric Ravilious and John Aldridge gravitated eastwards, joining Edward Bawden in Great Barden, Essex (before and after the war), as well as attaching themselves to Cedric Morris at Benton End in Hadleigh, Suffolk, just over the border, with John Nash living close by. Interestingly, both Bawden and Morris preferred to describe themselves as artist-plantsmen or artist-gardeners. There were writers' enclaves centred around George Barker and Elizabeth Smart at Tilty Mill, in Essex, or those around Randall Swingler in 'the People's Republic of Pebmarsh', a small Essex village, where artists and intellectuals such as Alan and Isabel Rawsthorne, Humphrey Searle, Paul Hogarth, Edgell Rickward, John Berger and occasionally Hedli and Louis MacNeice collected together at weekends, and where æsthetic principles and concerns were heatedly discussed.

Because so much of East Anglia is marshland and estuary, sky and water, the chromatic range on the east coast is quite different to that found elsewhere in Britain. Between them, Bawden and Ravilious found their ideal subject-matter in the county's ramshackle farm outhouses, smallholdings, and bleak winter fields, the former famously saying that the approach of spring filled him with horror, knowing that everything would turn green. Both preferred the browns, russets, mauves and muted colours of the furrowed fields, decoy ponds and fens of East Anglia in winter. In doing so, they created a sensibility — part æsthetic, part bloody-minded — that contributed an enduring element to the muscular style of 20th century English art. Time and again Sylvia Townsend Warner rhapsodised about the blues and greens of the marshes, while Paul Gallico asserted that 'greys and blues and soft greens are the colours, for, when the skies are dark in the long winters, the many waters of the beaches and the marshes reflect the cold and sombre colour.' In many ways winter is the season for this estuarine landscape, with its hundreds of thousands of migrant waterfowl, while inland 'it is just a curve of the earth, a rawness of winter fields,' according to now celebrated chronicler, J. A. Baker, prescient with 'always a sense of loss, a feeling of being forgotten.'

This predilection for the sculptural rather than the chaotic is vivid in Michael Ayrton's 1944 painting *Winter Drought*, where the brambles wrapping themselves around a dead tree trunk are indistinguishable in outline from barbed wire, whilst simultaneously evoking a cross of thorns. There is also a preference for the minimalist rather than the overripe, for a palette of muted colours evocative of the desert or the beach rather than the luscious and riotous colours of the exotic, all of which are now much more acceptable today in garden and landscape æsthetics. The sculptural elements of the forms to be found on the shoreline were recognised by Henry Moore, Barbara Hepworth and other artists in the 1930s, with John Piper writing in 1938 an intriguing essay 'Abstraction on the beach'. After the war, Prunella Clough made the East Anglian coast her own, explicitly rejecting the influence of Impressionism and dismissive of others' longing for Mediterranean light. She preferred 'the wind and the weather' of a self-professed northern European inheritance, concentrating at the outset of her long career on portraying the brute armature of the sea defences in *Closed Beach* (1945) and the irreducible forms of land, sea and skeletal remains in *Seascape and Bone* (1945), along with other depictions of a ruinous, windswept shoreline.

This shift from the interior to the eastern margins in imaginative territory happened in the second half of the 20th century, though the geographical locus of national identity was already on the move before then. For many, Shakespeare's birthplace in Stratford-upon-Avon was no accident, being 'seen as rooted in the geographical and linguistic heart of pastoral England,' according to historian Alun Howkins. In the early 20th century Hilaire Belloc and Edward Thomas 'created the world of the South Country and fixed it as a part of national ideology', noting that 'East Anglia was (and is) excluded from the ideal.' It could be argued that the need for an over-lush pastoral was a reaction against the blasted terrain of the Flanders battlefields occasioned by the First World War, and a reaction against the æsthetics of flatlands and prairie skies.

Subsequently Simon Schama argued that the upper Thames valley was the most frequently evoked geographical locus of Englishness, whether in the novels of Henry James, in spirited divertissements such as *Three Men in a Boat* and *Wind in the Willows*, or even in utopian tracts such as William Morris's *News from Nowhere*. The upper Thames from Hammersmith to Oxford constituted the very heart of English topographical perfection and, according to Schama: 'It supplied the prototypical image that was reproduced in countless paintings, engravings, postcards, railway train photographs, and war posters, which merely had to be executed to summon up loyalty to the temperate, blessed, isle.'

The Second World War changed all this. It reconfigured the political landscape along with attitudes towards topography, and the work of the late W. G. Sebald has proved particularly important to the re-imagining of the region. Sebald has woven East Anglia back into a European narrative, his writings emphasising the interconnectedness of the eastern shoreline with the dark sites of European history. The affinities and correspondences he teases out and interrogates in his travels and memories often begin and end at Liverpool Street Station, the gloominess of which suffuses several encounters in Sebald's peregrinations, reminding us that Pevsner had, many years before Sebald, attributed the lack of interest in Essex and beyond to the grim disincentive of this bleakest of London rail terminals.

Downriver, the Thames has played its part in global history too. For Joseph Conrad the river's wide estuary was both mysteriously beautiful but also 'one of the dark places of the earth', where Britain's imperial reach began, and where for a very long time the slave trade brought immense wealth to shipowners and traders. 'The conquest of the earth,' he wrote, 'which mostly means the taking it away from those who have a different complexion or slightly flatter noses than ourselves, is not a pretty thing when you look into it too much.' Places of departure are, however, also places of arrival: empire proved to be a two-way street. On 22 June 1948, a former German cruise ship, seized by the British at the end of the war and renamed MV Empire Windrush, brought 493 Jamaicans to Tilbury Port to start a new life in Britain, many of them encouraged to come to work in growing public services such as health and transport. In denial about the historic legacies of empire, the irony was honed into the quizzical observation that 'we asked for workers and got people'.

11 Landschaft and landskip

Landscape is neither backdrop nor allegory, but something dynamic, in between. Until the rise of modernism in æsthetics (and its cognate, existentialism in philosophy) the dominant way of representing landscape was as something separate and distinct from human activity. It had either been created by God as a setting for the unfolding of human destiny, or was employed as a visual framing device for various forms of morality pageant in the work of artists, dramatists and other writers. Thus the visual representation of landscape was privileged at the expense of the lived and felt experience of place. Hence the distant view, and the use of perspective to allow both the near and the far to be given equal prominence. The Claude glass, once used to 'frame' the perfect composition, was in the 20th century replaced by the view from the car window. Topographical publications were sponsored by petrol companies, and even suggested where to park in the landscape to get the most accommodating view. An even greater distancing mechanism is the rise of the aerial view, usually filmed in bright sunshine with scudding clouds casting shadows across the land, eventuating in a kind of soft pornography of place and affect.

Earlier chroniclers of rural life, labour, folklore and customs understood the connections between topography and economy, people and place — the working landscape. American landscape historian J. B. Jackson long ago argued that Daniel Defoe, John Evelyn, Arthur Young and William Cobbett were as interested in local customs, crafts, agricultural traditions, husbandry and religion as they were in the distinctive flora and fauna of the region, let alone its æsthetic beauty. This understanding was radically supplanted by a Romanticised view of rural life which became preoccupied with the effects of landscape on the spectator's sensibility rather than on the felt experience of those who lived and worked there. Geographer Denis Cosgrove locates this dichotomy in the etymological distinction between *landschaft* and *landskip*, landscape as custom and culture and landscape as pictorial representation.

The development of the Picturesque æsthetic in Britain, in conscious rejection of French and Italian formalism, retained an inherent social element in its early formulations, being seen to represent English freedom rather than Continental despotism. Yet even that rationale evaporated as the style became the province of the rich and powerful, happy enough on occasions to clear whole villages and woods in order to achieve a more 'natural' look. Landscape improvement, and subsequently æsthetic reception, became dominated by painterly and theatrical visual effects, dispensing with notions of utility or economy. Of William Kent, who started out in life as a painter, Walpole wrote that, in his designs, 'he realised the compositions of the greatest masters in painting.' Lancelot 'Capability' Brown said that his ideal was to make the 'English garden exactly fit for the Owner, the Poet and the Painter.' Humphrey Repton was distrusted by many throughout his life as being a showman, a man who used 'before' and 'after' sketches to sell his improvements to wealthy landowners, with one disillusioned estate steward complaining that Repton's proposals for Longleat amounted to nothing more than 'a Stage trick'.

This may be unfair to a canonical group of landscape designers whose influence continues to this day. It is certainly true that garden and landscape design is in its first intimations an exercise in sketching and the drawing of plans. Nevertheless, these men were designing what they regarded as private gardens, which such landed estates patently were, and whilst British garden design has continued to exercise a profound influence across the world, with regard to larger public landscapes in the 20th century the influences have mostly been the other way. Today we look to Dutch, American and Scandinavian landscape architecture for imaginative responses to the design of public landscapes, particularly where this involves large scale land reclamation, or the creation of new ecological parks on the sites of what was once contaminated industrial land. The English garden design tradition had problems in translating itself into a 21st century public works tradition, though Lutyens, Jekyll and the Jellicoes certainly had important successes in this field, particularly in projects involving memorialisation, notably with the Commonwealth War Graves Commission.

Yet there are even earlier, and still resonant, conventions by which our responses to the æsthetics of landscape and its cultural representation are framed and structured. The first artistic representations of landscape in western culture arrived in the form of miniatures: exquisitely painted illuminations found in early medieval Books of Hours. In his history of landscape art Kenneth Clark wrote of how the 'illumination' fused both subject-matter, the love of God, and an emotional mood through a suffusion of painted light, observing that 'it is no accident that this sense of saturating light grew out of a school of manuscript illuminations, and first appears in miniatures. For in such small images a unity of tone is more easily achieved, and the whole scene can be given the concentrated brilliance of reflection in a crystal.' The quality of light and what that light suggests in the way of divination or immanent meaning still haunts contemporary landscape painting and photography.

As religious paintings took on a larger canvas, more detailed landscapes emerged, often painstakingly painted as backdrops to the great Biblical stories. Intriguingly these landscapes often reflected the painter's homeland topography, thus producing the paradox that many of the seminal events in both Old and New Testaments, presumed to have taken place in the 'biblical lands' of the Middle East, ended up with European settings as *mise-en-scène*. Thus, to take some of the most famous examples of early religious paintings, Robert Campin's *The Nativity* (c. 1425) foregrounds the Bethlehem stable against a a verdant, meandering river valley, lined with a terrace of steep roofed medieval northern European brick houses, and Konrad Witz's *The Miraculous Draught of Fishes* (1444) is set against the shores of the lake of Geneva. *Crucifixion* (c. 1460) painted by Antonello da Messina 'with its dark sea and mountainous, irregular coast, clearly represents his native Sicily,' wrote Clark, while Patenier's richly coloured *Rest in the Flight into Egypt* (c. 1520) has a deeply wooded background, high gabled Dutch farmhouses, and Dutch peasants cutting golden fields of corn behind the Virgin and Child.

Closer to home, when William Dyce painted his portrait of an outcast Christ in the wilderness, *Man of Sorrows* (1860), the landscape depicted is the Scottish Highlands, The poet Kathleen Jamie has suggested that, along with a depiction of the personal desolation caused by rejection, the painting equally symbolises the emptiness caused by the Highland Clearances, which only ended in the 1850s. Not that these transpositions were regarded as anachronistic. This cultural translation helped to naturalise the Bible stories as vernacular tales, in addition to detailing, if not privileging, the domestic landscape. The play of light on hills, fields and villages, along with cloud formations, were exercises in mood (*stimmung*) as much as topographical realism. Desert stories were recast in northern forest clearings; colours were toned down and muted.

Paintings of the Crucifixion achieved their visual tension by uniting the vertical cross, and its human victim, with the horizontality of the landscape, an axial tension which continues to exert a dramatic hold on the western visual tradition to this day. This is memorably evident in the paintings of Caspar David Friedrich, or in that masterpiece of 20th century landscape architecture, the *Stockholm Woodland Cemetery* (1915–1961) by Gunnar Asplund and Sigurd Lewerentz (with its granite cross locking earth and sky together), as well as in Anthony Gormley's cruciform *Angel of the North* — three very different examples of this enduring morphological trope. It is also subtly evident in Kenneth Rowntree's admired watercolour, *The Livermore Tombs, Barnston, Essex* (c. 1940), one of his works for the 'Recording Britain' project, in which a distant telegraph pole with cross-member achieves a strong Friedrich-like cruciform effect in the distance.

Through repeated use and familiarity this verticality is now embedded within secular traditions of landscape representation. In photography there are commonly either 'landscape' or 'portrait' formats, neatly exemplifying the two axes. An understanding of this visual *axis mundi* — the axis by which the human presence establishes itself in the world — has always been a central component of landscape painting. The Norwegian architect and historian Christian Norberg-Schulz has written that 'the axis mundi is therefore more than a centre on earth; being a connection between the cosmic realms, it is the place where a breakthrough from one realm to the other can occur.' Thus the vertical is simultaneously the human and the sacred, earthbound, but reaching up towards the sky. This is what classically the minaret, the tower, the steeple and the cross in the landscape sought to symbolise; today, however, other emblems of human endeavour take their place. As to the horizontal axis, this is the plane of action, and, over time, of place and dwelling.

Where are the people?

This axis remains crucial to the representation of landscape, even in a modern, secular world. One of the challenges in documenting the landscape over a number of years has been representing what are today frequently isolated and depopulated places — where a strong vertical element is often missing — as places which were once settled and inhabited. Documenting absence is, after all, a common obligation for those engaged in forms of artistic representation which seek to honour those 'hidden from history' or who once belonged to 'worlds we have lost'. It is not surprising that such documentation tends towards horizontality, with what is lying below ground being as important as that remaining above.

Where are the people? The majority of those who settled and worked in these peninsular territories are long dead. Even those who currently live in coastal settlements are rarely found pacing the seawalls, traversing the empty yards of former factory complexes, or walking the marshlands in deep winter. The industrialisation of agriculture itself has produced its own eerie depopulation, as landscape historian Nan Fairbrother once observed, noting in a haunting phrase that even 'the animals are coming indoors.'

Yet evidence of human activity remains everywhere, whether in the exotic ballast flora growing in the vicinity of old ports and harbours, in the derelict jetties, cranes and warehouses of abandoned docks, in industrial ruins, in deserted asylums and hospitals, derelict boats, and a multitude of other *memento mori* of past lives and endeavours. The field systems themselves tell an epic story, according to historian Oliver Rackham, 'The modern development of south east Essex has all been inserted into a grid laid out nearly 2000 years ago.' Yet summoning up the past through these ancient patterns of pathways, green lanes, hedgerows, tree lines and field shapes requires attentive reading. What was once customary knowledge today requires a cultivated, historically conscious eye.

These ostensibly empty landscapes raise problems for those who seek to represent the social history of a region or a landscape when the people, along with their settlements and livelihoods, are no longer there. But traces always remain. In a critique of Ordnance Survey maps, writer Nick Groom focused on the absence of field names and church dedications in the maps themselves. His argument was that a whole way of life was commemorated in such names, including an annual round of rituals, fairs and festivals, and that this omission was clear evidence of the strategic military slant to this great scheme of cartography, along with a marked indifference to informal and popular forms of naming and commemoration.

Some of this 'empty geography' is the result of political decision-making, the most extreme case of which was patiently detailed by historian Patrick Wright in his classic work *The Village that Died for England*, an account of the forced evacuation of the small Dorset hamlet of Tyneham and its hinterland for military training prior to the Second World War. For more than a hundred years strategic areas of the Essex peninsula have also been in the hands of the military; at Rainham Marshes occupation dates back to the 18th century. Foulness Island remains unique in that it is home to a thriving community, who come and go as they wish, but is off-limits to outsiders. Elsewhere along the coast, areas of marshland and heath remain permanently closed to the public, whilst others are sealed off on a temporary basis during military exercises.

The red flag, signalling that the landscape is currently under military command, is a familiar sight still. Paradoxically this *cordon sanitaire* has offered protection for many birds and small mammals, as well as promiscuous vegetation. Such protection extends to a small seal colony often seen basking on the northern bank of the Pyefleet Channel, given sanctuary by the Danger Areas of Wick and Langenhoe Marshes, and apparently indifferent to the sound of automatic weapons being tested daily nearby. At first sight these common seals appear unusually orange-red in colour, and indeed they are, their pelts having accumulated large amounts of oxidised iron, and so they too take on the colouration of their local habitat.

This policy of territorial exclusion may in future no longer be justified solely on military grounds. For the purposes of nature conservation and protection, some parts of the Essex coastline and its smaller islands are only accessible according to a restricted timetable, frequently excluding visitors during the nesting season. Greater restrictions may yet occur. In the Netherlands, it is already government policy to designate certain wetlands as places of permanent public exclusion, in order that existing and reintroduced species may flourish.

The nature conservation area at Oostvaardersplassen, north of Amsterdam is a pioneering example of this strategy of 're-wilding'. Established as a successful conservation area in the 1980s, ponies and cattle have been reintroduced and left to fend for themselves, joining a wide variety of large birds including harriers, sea eagles and spoonbills, recreating a much older ecosystem, similar to that which existed prior to human intervention. It is likely that land devoted exclusively to wildlife conservation will form part of the landscape character of Britain in future years.

As to whether it will always be possible to find evidence of the past in the landscape, or whether in some places all memory and traces have been erased entirely (the true nightmare of George Orwell's novel *Nineteen Eighty-Four*), the jury of historians has yet to pronounce. Alexandra Walsham concludes her historical study of the impact of the Reformation on the English landscape by asking precisely this question, suggesting that while the material evidence may disappear, the record of human memory, story-telling and narrative ensures that some record will remain. 'Imprinted with our obsessions and values,' she writes, 'and moulded by selective erosion, amnesia, and invention, they (the landscapes themselves) are the products less of timeless natural processes than of human subjectivity.' Her patient account of the persistence of mythologies of place belies the adage that *scribere necesse est, vivere non est*: only that written really happened.

Nevertheless, along with the wish to live close to the land, traditions of local topographical writing and record keeping survive in many places. Geographer David Matless observed that in the 1930s and 1940s — as town dwellers began to explore the countryside — the idea was promulgated both by government and rural amenity groups that good citizenship involved learning the country code. Bird watching manuals along with pocket guides to flora and fauna helped cultivate the role of the amateur naturalist and citizen-geographer (though earlier cultures of self-taught erudition in geological and natural sciences were well documented by historians E. P. Thompson and Keith Thomas). The Victorian 'spade clubs', such as the group of amateur archæologists who opened up the Mersea Mount in 1912 to discover a Roman burial chamber within, have in more recent times been supplanted by the metal detectorists, often suffering unfair professional opprobrium, even though many of them have made important finds. Essex has benefited from such obsessive chroniclers.

The ecstatic prose of J. A. Baker (1926–1987) has given the county special status in the world of naturalist literature in recent times. Baker, a transport manager who lived and worked in Chelmsford for most of his life, was a keen birdwatcher, and spent much of his free time cycling in and around the Chelmer River and the Blackwater estuary recording its avian life. He retained, however, a particular, almost mystical, affection for — and identification with — the peregrine falcon. Baker was quite clear about the importance of familiarity and detail, writing at the outset of *The Peregrine* that 'one part of England is superficially so much like another. The differences are subtle, coloured by love.' The territory was small, but his imagination was immense, creating a world that was Shakespearean in atmosphere, drama and dizzying emotional extremes.

Less well known, but equally alert to the land and its seasons, was Loughton resident D. W. Gillingham, who in the late 1930s kept a journal, published in 1953 as *Unto the Fields*, an exquisite record of the woodlands, streams and rivers of the Roding Valley, close to Ching-ford, rich in bird life, small mammals and wild flowers, even though the streets of London's east end were less than ten miles away. From the hills of Loughton he claimed to be able to hear the roar of the London traffic, and even see the smoke from steamers on the Thames at Galleons Reach. Others may want 'scenery' he wrote, 'but the beauty of the English country-side is far less in its wide panoramas than in its intimate nooks and corners, in what lies so near at hand.'

Like Baker, Gillingham worked in an office ('uncongenial work'), escaping from the 'arid plain of failure' to cycle everywhere on his early morning or night-time forays into the Roding valley. In the published writings of both authors there is little mention of work, of domestic life or other interests — just an obsessive empathy with birds, and their migrations, nestings, feeding patterns and interaction with the rest of the natural world. From such patient obser-vations, we learn of the variety of life then to be found even in suburban lanes and by river-banks, in Gillingham's case, before the arrival of a barrage balloon station and a new housing estate. Gillingham's description of his adopted territory, which becomes a refuge from the world, recalls those wonderful passages in the early novels of D. H. Lawrence when that writer rhapsodised about the walk from his terraced street of miners' cottages in Eastwood to Hagg's Farm nearby, where 'a new life began in me'.

While full rein was given by such writers to the intimate detail of their observations, in other representations of the countryside censorship and self-censorship have always been at work. In her account of the 'Recording Britain' project, Gill Saunders observed that through-out the whole portfolio of more than 1,400 watercolours, 'cars appear occasionally, and here and there a distant pylon or a telegraph pole, but many scenes refused to acknowledge the 20th century.' The excision of signs and symbols of modernity and change is still evident in contemporary magazines portraying rural England. 'There are no pylons, mobile phone masts, new buildings or telegraph poles to be seen,' according to geographer Tim Edensor, who has made a study of these codes of representation. Photographers providing images for such publications are under strict instructions to ensure that such 'intrusions' remain out of view, even though rural life would be impossible without this infrastructure of public utilities and modern communications.

For the past hundred years or more the rural landscape has been marked by the con-struction of reservoirs, water towers and pumping stations, telephone lines, electrification schemes requiring power lines and pylons, generating sub-stations and, latterly, coal-fired, gas-fired and nuclear power stations. East Anglia has had all in abundance. With the excep-tion of a handful of modernist poets in the 1930s who proclaimed the beauty of pylons and power stations, these new architectural and engineering works have never been formally ab-sorbed into the æsthetic representation of rural life and landscape, and such omissions have substantially contributed to the confusion we experience today.

Capturing this palimpsest of past lives and changing landscapes is a key part of any new æsthetic, representing a formidable challenge to landscape photography. In the work of Fay Godwin and others, one can see these æsthetic dilemmas being addressed. There is today a growing body of photographic work producing images of almost geological intricacy and responsiveness to multiple traces of human dwelling. Within this genre a number of photographers are responding to the means by which we register absence as playing a shaping role in how we experience the modern world and the modern landscape. The absent has a geography too. The challenge for artists and others is how to represent it. The challenge for politicians, planners and developers is how to respect it.

Experiments in living

The former dense industrial landscape of east London remains imprinted on my childhood memories, especially the dark, forbidding docks and warehouses of the Pool of London, the river itself thick and bustling with ships and tugboats. Beyond the Royal Docks lay Beckton Gasworks, close to where the Northern Outfall Sewer — once described by David Corke as 'the largest tributary of the Thames' — reaches the river. Beyond that is Ford's at Dagenham, in Essex proper. Here one of the largest car factories in the world once operated with over 40,000 workers. Following the Thames heading eastwards there was Rainham Marshes, a former military training area complete with arsenals and firing ranges, then further along came the docks and liner terminal at Tilbury, the oil refineries at Corringham and Shellhaven, the fishing village of Leigh-on-Sea, Southend and on to the sequestered military lands of Foulness and the 'Essex archipelago'. The vast silver estuary, and much of coastal Essex, was busy with shipping.

This Essex foreshore is wholly a product of the modern world, including strategic areas of land reclaimed from the sea, as well as the fortuitous creation of vast swathes of former industrial and military land now lying unused and neglected. The latest of these great reclamation projects is the new London Gateway container port at Thames Haven, close to Stanford-le-Hope, where Joseph Conrad once lived. Financed and managed by Dubai Ports, London Gateway is scheduled to become one of the largest container ports in the world, handling ships capable of carrying up to 18,000 containers each. The new docks will be created entirely on new land, largely consisting of 30 million cubic metres of sand dredged from the English Channel as far north as Harwich. Currently under construction, the site achieves an epic scale, a limitless terrain of earthworks stretching as far as the eye can see, across mountains and valleys of sand, over which giant earth-movers slowly move backwards and forwards, clearing and levelling.

This today is the scale of landscape reconstruction required today by the global movement of goods. The size of the ships, the computer controlled cranes and monumental storage wharves now combine to form self-contained worlds in which the human scale is almost negated, and these landscapes now seem separate from human control or agency. The environmental price to be paid for such developments is not only high, but is recompensed elsewhere, by displacement. At Thames Haven more than 350,000 creatures, including over 40,000 newts, have been relocated to a large wildlife and wetlands habitat specifically created nearby as part of the planning deal.

Most land reclamation projects have been on a smaller scale, created principally for agricultural purposes rather than for industry or human settlement, though a number acted as precursors to various imperial colonisation schemes, as well as in the interests of social reform or 'moral renewal' at home. Essex has consistently played host to a variety of such endeavours, and in the late 19th and early 20th centuries the county witnessed a large variety of metropolitan social reform projects employing the vocabulary of the 'land colony', where, under strict conditions, or in a spirit of political zeal, new lives might be moulded. Thus some of the most radical as well as the most vulnerable inhabitants in London moved to Essex to start a new life on the land. These settlements included the Hadleigh Farm Colony (founded 1891, Salvation Army), Mayland Colony (1896, socialist), Purleigh Colony (1896, Tolstoyan anarchist), Ashingdon Colony (1897, Tolstoyan anarchist), Wickford Colony (1898, Tolstoyan socialist), and Laindon Farm Colony (1904, socialist/municipal). The eminent municipal socialist, George Lansbury, articulated this utopian spirit succinctly when, as leader of the Labour Party in 1934, he said that 'I just long to see a start made on this job of reclaiming, recreating rural England.' Even for the party of the industrial working class, the dream of a bucolic rural homeland — Merrie England — remained powerful.

Some of these pioneering settlements still retain remnants of their original form. The 'Great Experiment' at Mayland, on the River Blackwater, is today a collection of abandoned outhouses, overgrown glasshouses, former railway tracks and river piers, located to the east of the more recent and flourishing settlement of Lower Mayland. The original experiment was part of the wider 'back to the land' movement which at the time involved the energies of Fabian Society enthusiasts such as Lansbury, Joseph Rowntree and Joseph Fels. It was Fels who set up the Mayland colony, after meeting Thomas Smith, a former Manchester printer, who had already established a landholding there in 1896, subsequently buying 600 acres of farmland, which he divided up into 21 separate smallholdings. These were all to be made available to families wishing to start a new life away from the poverty of the city and, in some cases, from failed attempts to farm in the colonies, particularly Australia.

Joseph Fels was the American son of former eastern European immigrants, who had inherited a fortune from the manufacture of soap and who had come to England to embrace the Fabian cause. He was already an avid follower of the land economist Henry George, and had previously joined George Lansbury in establishing a land colony for unemployed men at Hollesley Bay in Suffolk in 1887. Within a few years of setting up, the Mayland experiment was growing its own food, producing its own meat and dairy products, and providing homes and a school along with other social amenities for the colonists. Moreover, it was able to export produce to other parts of the region through the establishment of a short rail link to a river jetty, where boats could moor at high tide and from there set sail around the coast. Visitors to the colony included Peter Kropotkin, Rider Haggard, Sidney and Beatrice Webb and Keir Hardie.

The death of Fels in 1914, and the outbreak of the First World War, ended the experiment in its original form, though the community survived and a number of the plot-holders managed to buy their smallholdings and continue to make a living in the settlement. Some of the walnut trees survive, as do many of the hawthorn hedges marking out the lanes and boundaries. The former railway track is now a straight dark tunnel of trees leading to the skeletal remains of the original jetty at the head of the narrow Mayland Creek, also known as Pigeon Dock.

On a recent visit, the long lines of abandoned glasshouses were in the process of being bulldozed to the ground. A strange emptiness was palpable in the surrounding lanes and fields, disrupted only by occasional swarms of Brent geese rising in a great clattering and barking cloud to wheel around in the sky before heading further upriver. On the seawall the footpath had been cordoned off for repairs, but work had been abandoned temporarily as a colony of slow worms had been found hibernating under the flagstones. When Richard Mabey returned to another of these pioneer settlements, the former plotland community at Laindon, he found oak, ash, hawthorn and hornbeam thriving, mixed in with roses, lilac, laburnum, and apple trees, evidence, 'that this was once a lively human community.'

A duty towards the land

The experiment at Mayland was no isolated affair. At Ashingdon and Wickford, closer to Mayland, followers of Tolstoy established smallholding settlements in 1897 and 1898 respectively. Most famously, manufacturer F. H. Crittall built a model village mostly in the modernist style for his workers at Silver End near Chelmsford in 1926, complete with farm, hotel, department store and sports centre. The settlement was entirely self-sufficient, with its own water supply and electricity generating scheme. In the 1930s Silver End was judged to be the healthiest village in Britain. The estate still stands.

Working the land in what the philosopher John Stuart Mill once praised as necessary 'experiments in living' was regarded as having not just political but spiritual value by many pioneers. The writer and Bloomsbury bohemian John Middleton Murry was involved in several Essex experimental agricultural communities, and wrote a book about this, *Community Farm*, published in 1952. His first project came about in 1933 when he set up a socialist community called The New Adelphi at Langham, north Essex. Murry's son Colin subsequently wrote that his 'own suspicion is that the Adelphi Centre owed its birth to D. H. Lawrence's *Pantisocratic Rananim* – that wistful dream of an ideal community where a chosen group of friends would live out their lives in perfect fulfilment.' Alas, such contentment was not to be. One probationary member, the anarchist George Woodcock, found the mix of people too volatile. 'Under the same roof were anarchists, left-wing socialists and secular-minded pacifists; there were Quakers, Plymouth Brethren, Catholics and one mild-mannered man who professed himself a Satanist; there were vegetarians, bicycle-club enthusiasts, Esperantists and nudists.'

As war approached, some of Murry's followers moved to Frating Hall Farm near Great Bentley, where they farmed 370 acres of mostly potatoes and cabbages, though they also managed 8,000 chickens. Most were pacifists and therefore conscientious objectors but, as farm workers, were eligible for 'conditional exemption' from military service. Vera Brittain was a shareholder in the farm and her daughter, the Liberal Democrat peer, Shirley Williams, worked there. In his account of these times Murry — once married to Katherine Mansfield, as well as being a close friend of D. H. Lawrence — wrote that, despite all the personal and political travails involved in these rural experiments, he believed that 'service to the land is an unconditional good', and that only agriculture offered the fullest opportunity for a developed sense of responsibility amongst people. Murry noted that 'work on the land is necessary to the life of man in a way no other work can be.' At the end of his somewhat anguished plea for a better post-war world he further declared that, 'what stands fast in the English countryside today is primarily, and almost solely, the duty towards the land.'

These scattered utopias, old and new, are mostly unmarked on the map, but remain strong in people's memories and in local history memoirs. Attachment to working the land, along with the physical benefits of life outdoors, still seems to provide a powerful impulse behind many utopian schemes. When walking the footpaths and seawalls one still comes across smallholders, riverboat dwellers, and others living and working 'on the margins': the land-scape would be bereft without these small experiments in living. They act as both a safety valve and a beacon in an economic system that has almost eradicated the language of liveli-hood and self-sufficiency from the political vocabulary.

Nevertheless, a farm is rarely a pretty thing, an organic farm perhaps even less so. There will be outbuildings in various states of disrepair, from different periods and made of differ-ent materials — timber, corrugated iron, concrete, brick, glass, steel and plastic. In the main yard there will be tractors, trailers, oil tanks, collections of gas bottles, amongst which chick-ens, sheep, dogs and cats will promiscuously mingle, padding between drinking troughs, improvised out of old sinks, and fed by a hosepipe run from a standpipe or the kitchen, tied to an upright drain with wire or string. There will be feeding troughs too. In the stable yard cows or horses will scatter hay as they come in and out of the fields, and casually excrete as they do so, creating pools of slurry. Muddy access roads will be heavily rutted and puddled, and constantly repaired with gravel, shingle or old pieces of plywood. Out in the fields and on the sea-wall, fences, gates and stiles will be improvised from old pallets, iron bed frames, steel tubing, wire netting, barbed wire, timber and plastic sheeting, secured by old dog leads, loose chains, orange or blue nylon twine, rope and cycle inner tubes. In the fields themselves, feeding and drinking troughs will be made out of old bathtubs and domestic water tanks, with room for rusting farm equipment, tyres and water pumps. A farm needs a variety of vehicles too: tractors, pick-up trucks, vans and trailers. The more the farm is self-sufficient, fashion-ing its buildings, fences and roads from the materials to hand, the less conventionally attrac-tive it is to outsiders. Working landscapes create their own æsthetics.

III A temporary arrangement with the sea

Just inside the churchyard gate of St Edmund King and Martyr, East Mersea, is a small burial mound, marked by a handmade wooden cross bearing the words, 'Unknown Person'. On first sight this tree shaded village church, painted by Rex Whistler during a respite from military training in June 1940, seems to exemplify English pastoralism, yet it is only a field away from where the North Sea meets the windswept estuary of the River Blackwater. St Edmund's was ministered by the Reverend Sabine Baring-Gould between 1870 and 1881, though he is better known as the author of the stirring hymns *Onward Christian Soldiers* and *Now the Day is Over*, and of the marshland gothic novel, *Mehalah: A Story of the Salt Marshes* about a man with so many children he could not remember their names.

Anonymous graves such as the one in St Edmund's churchyard are rare, and when found in coastal cemeteries usually indicate the burial of someone drowned at sea, whose body has been washed up unidentified. The *Friedhof der Namenlosen* in Vienna, the cemetery of the name-less, is devoted to those pulled dead from the Danube. There is a long tradition of respect and care afforded to such anonymous victims by maritime or riparian communities. Certainly, topography and mortality are interwoven, though it is not necessary to go as far as W. G. Sebald, who saw the whole world as one great cemetery.

It is difficult to imagine these near empty landscapes, occasionally punctuated by small settlements, as humanly bearable without the solace afforded by their churches, whether as beacons in the landscape or as quiet interiors. Looking across the northern estuary of the River Colne, at the confluence of the Blackwater and the Colne, lies Brightlingsea, where, in the churchyard of the larger and more prominent All Saints is the headstone and cenotaph of the Barber family:

IN LOVING MEMORY

CHARLES BARBER
AGED 46 YEARS
AND OF HIS SONS
THEODORE AND WALTER
AGED RESPECTIVELY 16 AND 14
WHO PERISHED WITH HIM AT SEA
SEPTEMBER 3RD 1884
ALSO OF HIS ELDEST SON
AGED 23 YEARS
WHO WAS DROWNED IN THE NORTH SEA
MARCH 6TH 1883
ALSO OF
AGATHA CAPON BARBER
WIFE OF THE ABOVE
WHO DIED OCTOBER 5TH 1920
AGED 84 YEARS

One's feelings here are not with the dead but the long widowed and child bereft survivor.

The West Tower of St Edmund's served as a lookout point and beacon during times of war, and the beaches, seawalls and fields all along this coast remain punctuated by concrete pill-boxes and fortified gun emplacements, many now covered with graffiti and moss. Some are disappearing beneath the sand as shore levels rise, as they do on the shingle spit leading to Mersea Stone. Others have been reduced to ruins by the sea. Such concrete outcrops are now as much a part of the Essex landscape as haybarns, feed hoppers and milking sheds. While some regard the pillboxes and tank-traps as a defacement of the landscape, others see them as a permanent reminder of the sacrifice made by others.

The debate about the retention of former military structures is a controversial topic elsewhere in Britain, as well as across the English Channel, where the proposed conservation of the 'Atlantic Wall' of German fortifications, now crumbling on the west coast of France, is setting one generation against another. For older people this long line of gun emplacements, bunkers and blockhouses represents a symbol of collaboration and defeat, whilst a younger generation feel that these brutalist installations are now a part of French history, not to be erased. 'We wouldn't for a minute consider destroying our mediæval castles,' one archæologist has said, 'but that is exactly what is happening to the Atlantic Wall, which is just as much part of our history.' For the French planner and architectural critic Paul Virilio, this great collection of concrete monoliths, watchtowers and murderous citadels has already moved from history into archæology, presenting a funerary monumentalism as significant as the Etruscan tombs or the Aztec ziggurats.

Mersea Island, meanwhile, has few claims to architectural or archæological fame, apart from one remaining Roman burial mound and the remains of several World War Two pill-boxes, gun emplacements and searchlight batteries. However, in 2006 the *Times Literary Supplement* reported that an American academic, Paul Streitz, arrived in Cambridge to give a lecture on the 17th Earl of Oxford and Elizabethan culture. During his talk he claimed that in 1604 Shakespeare 'was exiled to the island of Mersea in the English Channel', where he completed *The Tempest*. The island may not be quite as magical as it is in Shakespeare's play, but it does have a very special character of its own, and is just one of several inhabited islands off the Essex shoreline, in addition to around 30 uninhabited ones.

The latter number is as imprecise as the changing fractal mathematics of coastal landforms. Mersea itself is connected to the mainland by a permanent causeway known as the Strood. During high spring and autumn tides the island can be cut off from the mainland as the powerful estuary waters rush inland, covering the causeway road and filling the surrounding creeks, inlets and marshlands, so that the whole area resembles, even briefly, a stretch of open sea. When the tide abates the island roads are covered in seaweed and driftwood, reminding the visitor that one of the most distinctive features of this coastal fringe is that, in the words of ecologist David Corke, 'the most extensive and important habitats spend half the time under the sea.'

Anyone who writes about this coastal landscape has always to defer to Baring-Gould's *Mehalah*, the novel which did so much to create the atmosphere of isolation and mystery which surrounds the Essex marshlands. The opening pages are unsurpassed in their evocation of the haunting beauty of the marshland vegetation and the deep sense of loneliness which attends there:

> A more desolate region can scarce be conceived, and yet it is not without beauty. In summer, the thrift mantles the marshes with shot satin, passing through all gradations of tint from maiden's blush to lily white. Thereafter a purple glow steals over the waste, as the sea lavender bursts into flower, and simultaneously every creek and pool is royally fringed with sea aster. A little later the glass-wort, that shot up green and transparent as emerald glass in the early spring, turns to every tinge of carmine.
>
> When all vegetation ceases to live, and goes to sleep, the marshes are alive and wakeful with countless wild fowl. At all times they are haunted with sea mews and roysten crows, in winter they teem with wild duck and grey geese. The stately heron loves to wade in the pools, occasionally a whooper swan sounds his loud trumpet and flashes a white reflection in the still blue waters of the fleets. The plaintive pipe of the curlew is familiar to whose who frequent these marshes, and the barking of the brent geese as they return from their northern breeding places is heard in November.

In the novel the characters are as elemental a part of nature as the seabirds and dark swirling waters of the estuary and open sea. The shoreline is a place where human and natural forces meet, often dangerously, sometimes tragically, both in fiction and in life. Yet it is also a place of redemption and revelation, reminding us that human life and the natural world are part of the same order of things, mutually shaping and changing each other through space and time.

Refuge and prospect

A map of Essex is like a Rorschach test, or one of those ambiguous images used by psychologists to mirror the mind. Many first discern a solid landmass — roughly in the shape of a pentagon — criss-crossed by a network of major and minor roads. A minority note a richly convoluted coastal edge, penetrated by a series of estuaries and rivers, with the Thames marking the southern edge of the county and the Stour forming the border to the north. In between, the rivers Roach, Crouch, Blackwater and Colne reach deep into the flat, mostly arable countryside, softened by beaches, salt marshes and mudflats at the edges. Saxton's exquisite 1576 map of Essex highlights the country's complex river systems and eastern littoral, the true arteries and highways of the county at that time.

The irregularly infiltrated and islanded shoreline is special to Essex, and, like all coastal edges, a place of great ecological and cultural importance: a 'liminal' space in anthropological terms, a border territory where the rules of classification as to what belongs to the land and what to the sea are ambiguously interwoven. The intertidal zone — extending a mile or more from shore in some places — reveals how vast an area is exposed at low tide. Not only are the salt marshes, mudflats and sandbanks under water for half the time, but the shoreline too contains so many inlets, creeks and tiny archipelagos of marshland that the 'space' of the shoreline seems infinitesimally complex and unmeasured.

The border zone between land and sea has historically been an in-between space, where questions about one's place in the world come unbidden, an exposed terrain offering both a sense of freedom but also uncertainty and danger. The fixity of the land is challenged and even mocked by the dangerous unmanageability of the sea. For the Darwinist school of evolutionary landscape psychology, this would be a classic refuge/prospect configuration. The volatile conditions of the sea act as a continuous reminder of a growing and threatening imbalance between sea and land, as the world's climate alters in response to changing economies, technologies and demographic demands on natural resources. It is also, almost uniquely, a place to which public access is enshrined in common law and parliamentary legislation, thus possessing exceptional attributes in terms of landscape typology, reinforcing the political importance of the public domain as a place of shared rights and responsibilities.

Coastal landscapes are particularly distinctive, being in a state of constant flux. The tides which inundate the Essex shoreline, daily submerging the land beneath three to six metres of water, change the shape, colour and look of the terrain by the hour, as in a landscape of clouds and mirrors. In *Mehalah*, Baring-Gould described this prospect as one 'of debatable ground contested by sea and land,' and the Blackwater marshes represented the principal agent of destiny in his novel. The same was true for Joseph Conrad, notably in the opening pages of *Heart of Darkness*, where the 'benign immensity of unstained light' in the evening estuary sky, suffused by marshland mist, is contrasted to the unnatural gloom to the west, setting the scene for the moral catastrophe to come. The same mists and bird thronged river estuaries provided the shimmering underscore to Benjamin Britten's *Four Sea Interludes* and *Curlew River*. The emotions stirred by this fluidity are largely foreign to those living in the rural interior, or even by the Baltic or the Mediterranean, where tideless seas lack the emotionally powerful and destabilising effects which tidal shores offer — along with an ever present sense of danger and potential catastrophe.

Coastal settlements, and their inhabitants, therefore live by a different clock. 'Their changing magnitude and regularity,' historian Barry Cunliffe once wrote of tides, 'add a different measure of time, both complex and subtle, to the day-night cycle, and the changing seasons. Daily observance of tidal rhythms greatly enhances a community's awareness of the nature of time and its passage.' Overnight, roads and landforms appear and disappear, as they do daily along the Essex coast, where some of the smaller island causeways are useable for only a limited amount of time each day, before disappearing beneath the flood. In Arthur Ransome's novel *Secret Water*, based on Horsey Island in Hamford Waters, older sister Titty responds to Nancy's question as to what tides are for by saying 'it's like breathing. Up and down. Up and down. It makes everything alive.'

Crossing the causeway to Horsey Island is an unnerving, almost hallucinatory experience. One has to be quite certain of the tides and not go by the appearance of low water alone as a guarantee of safety. Unusually, the causeway is below the level of the adjacent riverbed, so one is driving almost at eye level with the mudflats and flowing watercourses on either side, where the waders seem almost unperturbed, making it possible to pass within six feet of a curlew or cluster of elegantly crested lapwings. The traveller shares the terrain at their level and as equals. Although the causeway is constantly repaired by the island's resident farmer — Horsey Island itself is a wildlife sanctuary and off limits to visitors for part of the year — the drive is a white-knuckle ride from side to side and up and down through the potholes and small residual seawater ponds left by the tide.

Islands possess distinct topographical and psychological qualities, both to those who dwell on them or those who view them from afar. They can be places of idyllic retreat — think of Ingmar Bergman's early film of first love *Summer With Monika*, or Tove Jannsen's childhood idyll *The Summer Book* — or of banishment and exile, as in *Robinson Crusoe* or the grim island prisons which have been used throughout history for those regarded as the most dangerous of social or criminal intransigents. They are also zones of fearful experimentation, as in H. G. Wells' monstrous *The Island of Dr Moreau*. On the other hand, they have distinct ecological advantages, as Darwin discovered in the Galapagos Islands, where it was the small differences between the finches on the separate islands which first alerted him to the principle of adaptation. Skipper Island and Horsey Island in the Walton Backwaters are protected for their unique habitat characteristics, and Mersea Island itself has some important role in this regard too. Staying at a rented cottage on the island in March 2013, I looked out of the kitchen window early one cold, bright morning, to see a red squirrel perched on the fence a few feet away. I subsequently found out that the grey squirrel, which elsewhere in the UK had largely displaced the red, never made it on to Mersea Island, and that, in 2012, several breeding pairs of red squirrels had been set loose in an experiment to reintroduce the species.

The islands of Essex have also served a role in the moral rehabilitation of people, whether it be Osea Island near Maldon, where conscience stricken brewer Frederick Charrington founded a Temperance Hotel — later adapted as sanctuary for those with addiction problems — or on Canvey Island where 'The Girls' Bungalow', otherwise known as the Social Institute, was established by Miss Clara James in 1909 (who later founded the Labour Party on the island) as a holiday home for working girls from east London. Canvey was also the setting for Hotel Ozonia, a temperance and fresh air settlement, which in 1938 advertised over 60 rooms available for healthy recuperation. Less benignly, Bramble Island in Hamford Water has been used for developing, testing and storing explosives, and for more than a hundred years Foulness Island has been sequestered for weapons development and testing by the military, its indigenous community at times isolated from the wider world, so much so that the women of Foulness wore Dutch costume as normal attire until the First World War.

The Great Tide

There was no warning of the great tide on the night of 31 January 1953, which cost so many lives in East Anglia. The winds were stronger than usual, but off the east coast the sea seemed relatively calm and lit by a full moon. A few people later recalled something odd that day. A police constable wondered why the afternoon tide on the River Blackwater didn't appear to ebb, noting afterwards that 'the wind seemed to be holding the water.' A few hours later the 7.27 evening train from Hunstanton to King's Lynn ran into a wall of water and was hit full on by 'a bungalow floating on the crest of the wave', an alarming incident which prefigured the catastrophe ahead.

That night over 300 died. In the Netherlands more than 1,800 lost their lives. Most, in the words of one survivor, 'awoke to die', trapped in bed as the waters filled their rooms, with little time or opportunity to escape. The tragedy was a reminder of how much the East Anglians and the Dutch shared in common. 'God made the world, but the Dutch made the Netherlands', it was said. They made large parts of East Anglia too.

As a child I lived on Canvey Island, our family moving to the mainland a year before the flood. At carnival time islanders dressed in Dutch costume, and many street names — Vadsoe Road, Zuyder Road, Delft Road and Kamerdyk Avenue — reinforced the connection. Our bungalow was in Grafton Road, which, like many Canvey roads, was a muddy lane, no more than 200 yards from the sea-wall, and typical of the flimsy houses which sprouted up between the wars along the Essex coast, where land was cheap. Our single-storey timber bungalow rested on brick piers, with a verandah at the front reached by open wooden stairs. Years later, Dr Feelgood's Wilko Johnson claimed these dwellings provided the authentic delta experience necessary for the Canvey Island delta blues.

The 'villain of the piece' that night was later identified as Low z, a depression which later merged with an older depression, Low k, south of Iceland, and swept eastward across Britain, followed by High a, a ridge of high pressure. The resulting northerly gale 'was such that there is no evidence in the records of the Meteorological Office of any equally severe.' Some good did emerge from the catastrophe, however. There was widespread public appreciation of the selflessness of those who rescued others that night, often at risk to their own lives. The emergency services, voluntary organizations, churches and thousands of individuals rose to the occasion. Flood defences were improved, and, in time, the disaster produced one of the great works of 20th century English social history, Hilda Grieve's epic narrative, *The Great Tide: The Story of the 1953 Flood Disaster in Essex*, published in 1959.

This vast documentary work of 900 pages combined meteorological detail, weather and topographical maps, oral history, official records, photographs, written testimony, entries from emergency service incident books, and much else. However, at its heart Grieve deployed a minute by minute narrative of the events of that night, from the moment the waves started to overtop the seawall at Sandilands in Lincolnshire at 5.25 pm until hours later when high tide arrived at Canning Town and the Port of London to complete its destruction. So vulnerable to disruption were communications at this time that many further up the coast were already dead, and their communities destroyed, whilst along the Thames, people slept soundly, unaware of what was about to hit them.

Street by street, Grieve systematically itemised the chaos of the disaster as it unfolded. By midnight, thick clouds obscured the moon and the sea had not only broken through the main sea defences but was now approaching from the swollen rivers and flooded fields behind, trapping people. This happened at Jaywick, a pre-war plotland development tucked behind a high seawall, where 35 people died, unable to escape in any direction. Not everybody drowned. Many died of the cold, perched on the roofs of their houses, waiting in the dark, lashed by wind and water, dressed only in their nightclothes. 'Some,' wrote Grieve, 'collapsed with the intense cold and shock and slipped down from places of safety into the water. Children died quietly of exposure in their parents' arms as they tried to hold them, hour after hour, above the water.' One mother later recalled of her son that 'after a while he did not speak any more and appeared to go to sleep.'

On Canvey Island, once the floods had subsided, bodies were collected from hedgerows and ditches and laid out on the pavement for identification. Mickey Sanders, a fireman, remembered laying out a row of 18 corpses on a Canvey pavement. 'They were all people I actually knew. You can't imagine what it was like.' Such images were never shown in the newspapers or on television, though the carcasses of more than 46,000 farm animals floating in the sea became a familiar icon of the tragedy.

What Grieve could not then calculate was the degree to which the 'spontaneous mobilisation' of help and relief she praised owed its swift effectiveness to organisational links and affiliations developed during the war, which had ended only eight years before. Britain was still a society of small platoons: civil and coastal defence bodies, army reserves, unionised railway workers and seamen, the Women's Voluntary Service, the Red Cross, St John's Ambulance Brigade, Boy Scouts and Girl Guides, churches, parish guilds and social clubs had all to an extent been militarised during the war, and inducted, however briefly, into the mechanics of disaster relief. From Grieve's account, almost every East Anglian appeared to belong to an organization whose loyalties and resources could be called upon in an instant without demur.

The new Essex which emerged from the catastrophe and subsequent years of reconstruction was described in the introduction as 'a walled fortress.' No longer. In East Anglia, as in the Netherlands, rising tide levels mean it is impossible to deflect the sea on every occasion. 'Managed retreat' is the new strategy, creating breaches in the seawalls and diverting flood waters into uninhabited marshland (at the same time, creating new wildlife habitats). Residential communities, such as those on Foulness and Canvey islands, still require traditional sea defences, but breaches along the less inhabited coastal areas prevent the creation of funnels, which cause high tides to gain speed and direction as they surge further inland.

The empire of nothingness

Long-term ecological concerns — as well as more immediate threats of serious flooding and loss of life — are highlighted by shoreline landscapes, the water's edge acting as a moral theatre or *paysage moralisé*. Two paintings of the seashore which have haunted the European imagination are pertinent here, capturing as they do that sense of loss and emptiness which seemed to arrive unexpectedly on the 19th century seashore: David Caspar Friedrich's *A Monk by the Sea* (1808–1810), where belief in the majesty of nature turns into doubt and apprehension, and William Dyce's *Pegwell Bay* (1858–1860), perhaps the most famous British Victorian painting of its time. This latter work, ostensibly recording the appearance of Donati's comet in the sky, is a painting in which the bare cliffs dominate, the tide is out, and a great feeling of vacancy and disenchantment fills the canvas (and therefore the world). God has gone elsewhere, leaving only bare geology and a handful of small figures collecting fossils, with a child standing awkwardly on the sand staring aimlessly into the middle distance. The beach became a new site of revelation, where previously it had been the desert, the wilderness, or on the mountain peak where religious belief was tested, and human self-knowledge attained. The exposure of the fossil record on the shoreline created a new site of existential anxiety.

This belief that it is only on the coast that the enigmas of human existence — and our ambiguous place in the natural world — are fully exposed, was the subject some years ago of Alain Corbin's great study *The Lure of the Sea*. The original French title of this book was *Le territoire du vide* (literally translated, 'The Territory of the Void', or, more poetically, 'The Empire of Nothingness'), more correctly capturing the anxiety which is the true subject of his great work. Corbin analyses the littoral as a place of revelation, alluding to the terrors of the deep waters, the atavistic fear of sea monsters and drowned sailors, and the mixture of unease and desire people feel when standing at the water's edge, reflecting on the insignificance of earthly life, brief as the scattering waves which collapse in on themselves before they reach the shore.

In Britain the most famous expression of this sense of human disenchantment evoked by the tidal shore comes in Matthew Arnold's poem *Dover Beach*, written in 1867, where he describes how the disparate sounds of the waves, drawing down and flinging back the pebbles on the seashore at night,

...bring
The eternal note of sadness in.

Sophocles long ago
Heard it in the Aegean, and it brought
Into his mind the turbid ebb and flow
Of human misery; we
Find also in the sound a thought,
Hearing it by this distant northern sea.

One of the more enquiring contemporary religious movements — inspired by the work of theologian, Don Cupitt — calls itself 'Sea of Faith', after a line in Arnold's poem. This theology-without-God seeks to counter the pessimism of the poem with a belief that, though God and supernaturalism have deserted the world, the role of faith continues.

At the tide's ebb, there can be an overwhelming sense of emptiness in a world bereft of meaning, growing in severity over time as scientific evidence began to question the divine nature of Creation. The novelist John Fowles once wrote of the loneliness of the Dengie peninsula in Essex, and its 'God-denying skies'. The period Corbin wrote about was an era in which geology was undermining traditional Biblical accounts of the origins of the world, revealing the role that marine organisms and sea creatures played in evolution. 'People,' he wrote, 'came to the coasts to browse in the archives of the Earth.' We now know, from bones found along the Essex coast, that bears, elephants and hippopotamuses once walked these shores.

This sense of wonder at the edge of things is plainly evident in children when they first encounter the sea. There is no landscape in the world as magical — or whose spaces are so immeasurable — as a tidal beach. As Corbin, again, was early to point out, 'in Greek literature, every boundary zone is a dangerous area in which the activities of deities, human beings, and animals, living in confused, dangerous proximity, threaten to interfere with one another.' The seals seen offshore or in the estuaries seem to belong to this ambiguous world. Thus the boundary between the land and the sea still remains a place where our beliefs and understanding of the sharp divisions between the categories of things becomes amorphous. Even the land, the sea and the sky blend into each other in unstable measures.

The shoreline is thus the antithesis of the sacred grove. The latter is a secret, enclosed space known only to the gods and their self-elected worshippers. It is a powerful spatial configuration which starts with the clearing in the forest, or the woodland glade, and over time is transmuted into the interior of the Gothic cathedral. By contrast, the transfigurative powers of the shoreline are boundless and summoned together on a temporal basis. Gathering at the water's edge became part of a more nonconformist tradition of religious congregation, as places where belief could be celebrated by those excluded from buildings which celebrated religion as a form of wealth and power. Even today religious groups can be found assembling and worshipping on the beach at Southend at weekends, a tradition that now goes back more than a hundred years. Baptism by immersion was once part of that.

There are further positive aspects to this moral and topographical drama. The sea is a symbol of freedom of movement as well as spiritual freedom: to set sail is to leave the past behind and travel in the hope of better fortune. It also represents escape from the confines of the deep interior, a boundless domain that has neither walls nor border guards. 'Man,' Byron wrote, 'marks the earth with ruin — his control / Stops with the shore.' Though such romance about the sea has largely disappeared, the shoreline remains a realm of freedom, and the sea itself is in the main regarded as communal territory, quite distinct and separate from terrestrial concepts of nationhood or proprietorial interest, though it too is now mined and exploited almost as much as the land.

Access to the greater part of the English coastline is today guaranteed by law, a freedom not available in other countries of the world where the privatisation of the foreshore is common. The Countryside and Rights of Way Act 2000 includes in its definition of 'open country' — that is to say, land that is publicly accessible to all — 'foreshore and land adjacent to the foreshore, including cliff, bank, barrier, dune, beach or flat adjacent to the foreshore'. A common right is accorded to any individual who wishes to fish in the sea or tidal waters, a right not extended to most inland waters. Even more recently, in its proposals for implementing the Marine and Coastal Access Act 2009, Natural England state their founding premise that, 'having arrived at the coast, people should normally be able to walk in either direction for as long as they like around the open coast of England.'

IV Modern nature: art, ecology, landscape

It is vital that the unassimilated landscapes described in this essay are documented and valued if they are not to be levelled or 'improved' in the name of some larger political programme. One of the most persuasive critics of the rush to eradicate all memory of the past is environmentalist and theologian John Rodwell. In his 2006 Reckitt lecture, 'Forgetting the land', he spoke of the coalfields of the Dearne Valley where his grandfather started work in the mines at the age of ten. When Rodwell went to the National Mining Museum seeking archive information about his grandfather's work record, he was told that 'all filing cabinets with all their records, furniture, office buildings and all the other superstructures of a colliery were bulldozed into the shaft.' These shafts were then capped, and in the case of his grandfather's pit, Cortonwood, it 'disappeared as if it had never existed.'

This obliteration of the past was captured by photographer John Davies in two photographs of Easington Colliery in County Durham. The first, taken in 1983, showed a large industrial complex at work, set close to the sea, surrounded by farmland. This was a classic mining landscape, in which the industrial and the pastoral coexisted alongside each other. The same site, photographed in 2004, shows rough grassland, levelled and barren. Rodwell rightly challenges those landscape projects which deny 'former trails of painful happenings, broken promises, unfair demands', reminding us that 'the ethics of memory are primarily concerned with the relationship between forgetting and forgiving.' The ancient curse, recorded by George Borrow in his travels in Wales, is brought to mind: 'may the grass grow in your streets'.

The relationship between remembering and forgetting is, paradoxically, related to the relationship between memorials and ruins. Novelist Robert Musil published an essay on 'Monuments' in 1936, noting how much of his native city of Vienna was crowded with memorials to soldiers, statesmen and illustrious figures, forgotten ever after. 'There is nothing in this world as invisible as a monument,' he wrote. Ruins, by contrast, are a reagent of memory, their incomplete, fractured elements demanding to be visualised or imagined whole again. Ruins invoke empathy and the free play of historical query, where memorials close the lid firmly and decisively on the past. In recent years, the de-historicization of both rural and urban landscapes, as a result of building development and urban renewal, has spontaneously occasioned a return to older practices of informal memorialisation. The roadside shrines commemorating victims of street accidents and other violent deaths, along with the widespread practice of placing commemorative trees, benches, or other markers (including the scattering of cremated remains) at places associated with those remembered, often in view of the sea, clearly suggest that a re-inscription of the landscape, a new counter-reformation, is underway.

Such informal modes of reclamation and inscription imply that landscape design needs to articulate site-specific, historical references when it comes to bringing land formerly used for military, industrial or other purposes back into public use. Swiss landscape architect Georges Descombes — who has designed a number of parks and memorial landscapes — has written of the need to restore older landscape structures to the surface again, writing of his approach to the design of a new park on a former industrial site at Lancy in France that it is intended to 'reveal its energies, the forces which shape it: folds, slopes, streams. Upon this wounded, haggard territory forms are born again, rising up and resisting all levelling down.' All landscapes are force fields when understood in this way, their latent energies released by sympathetic articulation.

Elsewhere in the world, progress on re-imagining and bringing back former industrial landscapes into public esteem is now advanced — as is a respect for the public memory of the sites concerned. Where landscape students used to travel to Stourhead in Wiltshire, Vaux-le-Vicomte in France, or the Boboli Gardens at Bomarzo in Italy to admire the work of the great masters, today's more adventurous trainees are encouraged to visit Gasworks Park on the shore of Lake Union in Seattle or the Landschaftspark created on the site of the former steelworks in Duisburg-Nord, close to the Ruhr. In Seattle, visitors clamber over rusting retorts and towers or join fellow picnickers on the undulating green sward covering industrial spoil, looking out to ageing jetties where cargo boats once docked. In Duisburg, strollers climb the 350 foot narrow, iron-caged ladder to the top of the blast-furnace chimneys or venture along catwalks overlooking the shunting yards. These have been planted as orchards, from where one can watch diving club members descend into the black waters of the former coal bunkers, now flooded. At Crissy Field in San Francisco, landscape architect George Hargreaves has redesigned a former military base as a new national park, which also functions as a public exercise in hydrological and ecological renewal; while at the gargantuan Freshkills landfill site on the edge of New York City, James Corner Field Operations have embarked on a 30 year plan to remodel this vast terrain of toxic rubbish as yet another national park. Successful transformations such as these possess enormous educational and political resonance.

These programmes of landscape restoration and design owe much to the land art movement of the 1960s, particularly to the work of American artist Robert Smithson, who was attracted to and energised by the bleak wastes created by suburban sprawl, mineral extraction and rusting industrial machinery. What to others appeared static and ugly, Smithson saw as being in a constant process of entropy — even the new buildings going up he saw as ruins in the making. Land could be shaped in and around the remains of what had gone before to create settings on a more epic, geological scale. Hence his spirited æsthetic credo: 'the ice age rather than the golden age'. Hence, too, the title of the first exhibition he curated in New York in 1968, 'Earthworks', its name suggested by the title of a novel he had read the previous year by British science fiction writer, Brian W. Aldiss. 'Don't underestimate dirt,' two co-contributors to the 1968 'Earthworks' exhibition, Michael Heizer and Walter De Maria, telegraphed their art dealer.

This recourse to a different scale of time suggested that art and nature might find a new rapprochement. In 1969 Smithson and his wife Nancy Holt travelled extensively in England and Wales, fascinated by ancient standing stones, barrows and geological findings which they researched and photographed obsessively. During the period of Smithson's explorations, French historian Ferdinand Braudel was suggesting that history operated within three concurrent orders of time: biological time, social time and geographical time. Biological time was that experienced in an individual lifetime; social time was the longer historical and cultural context in which different generations lived and understood their place in history; geographical time was the slow cyclical time of the geological and natural world. People occupy all three time frames simultaneously. A designed landscape could, if properly conceived, weave all three together. Yet some landscape management practices seek to freeze time, and resist geological change, in the name of a fixed æsthetic. When Yew Tree Tarn in the Lake District began to empty as a result of a geological fault, the National Trust spent heavily repairing the fault, so that the beauty of the tarn would be 'permanent'.

The year before Smithson's New York exhibition, English artist Richard Long created a work called A Line Made by Walking (1967), in which he walked up and down a suburban field continuously, creating a straight line of flattened grass, which was then photographed. From this he developed the idea of walking as an artistic intervention, annotated or not, as he variously carried pebbles from one side of the country to another, created stone circles in remote places, and in other discreet ways re-energised the force fields of the natural terrain. Long was later to write that 'my art is always about working in the wide world, wherever on the surface of the earth. My art has the themes of materials, ideas, movement, time. The beauty of objects, thoughts, places and actions.' While most live in cities today, many of our most prescient imaginings are located in wilder, elemental places, evoking Samuel Beckett's stage directions for Waiting for Godot: 'A country road. A tree. Evening'.

The idea that such essaying out into the world could in itself constitute a work of art was not new. Robert Macfarlane has described how the poet Edward Thomas developed a series of one-day walks which involved either consistently turning to the left or to the right at any junction, thus creating small or larger circular itineraries which would eventually return him home. Eric Ravilious considered mapping all the places where he had kissed his first sweetheart. Before them the German essayist Robert Walser, published his novella The Walk in 1917, inspiring a whole generation of artists to put their walking shoes on in search of serendipitous experiences and visual treats. In many ways Smithson's famous 1967 essay, 'A Tour of the Monuments of Passaic, New Jersey', reprises Walser's walk, as the young American artist wandered round his suburban home town, visualising the pumping derricks, bridges, play equipment and pylons as 'found' monuments in what others regarded as a degraded, unæstheticised landscape.

A growing number of writers have since returned to exploring the terrain on foot — a grouping in which W. G. Sebald and Iain Sinclair have been exemplars — giving rise to what is becoming a new kind of secular pilgrimage, based on the principle of immersion. For 'the path' or 'the way' is both a spiritual construct as well as a spatial one: walking combines the two. 'They only know a country who are acquainted with its footpaths,' wrote Richard Jefferies.

Et in Arcadia Ego

Two British artists have achieved international status in the field of landscape design: Ian Hamilton Finlay and Derek Jarman. For personal reasons Finlay remains special to me because, in 1996, I went to interview him at his isolated house, Little Sparta, in the Scottish borders, for a book I was writing about memorial landscapes. It was an exceptionally cold January afternoon, and many smaller roads were snowbound. The walk from the hired car took me across several fields, the paths and ditches of which had been obliterated by snow, so much so that I was worried I might lose all sense of orientation in the entirely white landscape, with night coming on. The return walk in total darkness was even worse.

In Finlay's work, word puns, elegant typography, and a printmaking technique based on picture-book style images and words create a childlike wonder at the connection between words and things. The tension between pictures and labels, images and text, was also at the heart of linguistic philosophy in the 20th century, and Finlay nearly always described himself as a philosopher-poet rather than an artist. A growing interest in the place of inscription — especially in the landscape, often reworking the motifs embodied in Poussin's paintings of *Et in Arcadia Ego* — made him better known in Europe than he was in his own country.

Even before his death, it was recognised that the garden at Little Sparta was his greatest work of art. There are few modern designed landscapes in Europe which have not incorporated elements of Finlay's vision of a world made new by reference to the old. Formalism, inscription, the melding of the natural with the sculptural and the architectonic, returned to favour, largely owing to the influence of Finlay, controversial though his allusions and apparent allegiances to the iconography of violence and terror — in the midst of classical calm — remained. Finlay was thoughtful, serious and kind on the occasion I met him, though he employed a vocabulary of politics and art that was entirely foreign to me then, less so now. Central to this vocabulary was the notion of piety. For Finlay, as for Edmund Burke before him, the sublime was an unnerving admixture of beauty, order and terror, and not for the faint hearted nor the corporate piazza. This emphasis on piety reminded me of a claim made by some environmentalists that people only respect landscapes which contain a significant element of danger. Since the English landscape largely lacks these things, other means of inducing a degree of fear and trembling might be needed or sought: melancholy inscription, admonitory messages of life's brevity. Some find this in churchyards and cemeteries. *Et in Arcadia Ego*.

Jarman's work was altogether different. The garden he created around his cottage on a shingle beach at Dungeness was designed and constructed from an accretion of found materials and indigenous vegetation. All this was achieved in the shadow of a nuclear power station, and in the midst of an idiosyncratic collection of old fishermen's huts and ageing weekend holiday chalets, previously regarded as inhospitable and ugly terrain. In his diaries he described telling artist Maggi Hambling about the project:

> I was describing the garden to Maggi Hambling at a gallery opening. And said I intended to write a book about it.
> She said: 'Oh, you've finally discovered nature, Derek.'
> I don't think it's really quite like that, I said, thinking of Constable and Samuel Palmer's Kent.
> 'Ah, I understand completely. You've discovered modern nature.'

Modern nature: human settlement, ecology, history and æsthetics in one strange assembly. The garden was not only beautiful but, for Jarman, was a 'therapy and pharmacopoeia'. He recycled old timber, rusting metal, ropes and other flotsam, studied the flowers and vegetation of the shingle beach for their visual and herbal properties, inscribed a poem on the flank wall of the wooden cottage, and created a magical environment that was both an artwork and an exercise in ecological exegesis and conservation. His notebooks are filled with the names of dozens of plant species, lichen and mosses found on the beach, which he cultivated ornamentally, whilst noting the many different birds which came to the garden. There was a beehive too.

There are lessons here for the sympathetic recuperation and re-enchantment of some of the most blighted landscapes. The nature reserve at Fingringhoe on the River Colne, created by the Essex Wildlife Trust on the site of former gravel and sand extraction pits, is much loved and much visited. There, in high summer, nightingales populate deep avenues of blackthorn and hawthorn and fill the air with constant birdsong; adders can be seen dozing on vacant stretches of sand between large swathes of yellow gorse (with its heady smell of coconut). These wildlife reserves are the successors to the earlier land colonies, speaking to a contemporary need to imagine life whole again, human settlement and the natural world undivided.

Canvey Wick, on Canvey Island in the Thames Estuary, often considered one of the ugliest settlements in Britain, is now described as 'England's little brown rainforest', supporting 'more biodiversity per square foot than any other site in the UK.' Another nature reserve has been established on Two Tree Island, a former landfill site, close by. Today it is richly vegetated and serene. The eastern edge of the island faces on to a series of brackish lagoons which have become an important breeding ground for avocets. At Rainham Marshes, an estuarine landscape lit by a kaleidoscope of cloud, sky and water converging on the Thames as it bends at Erith Rands, another wildlife sanctuary has been created on a former collection of military firing ranges and ordnance depots close to Dagenham. There the RSPB has brought to fruition a rich marshland environment, to which birds arrive from many parts of the world. The landscape is also home to large colonies of marsh frogs, voles and other water creatures. The complex network of boardwalks, bridges, bird hides and viewing platforms designed by architect Peter Beard has a strong philosophical basis in the art of pathfinding and memory of place, weaving in references to prehistoric brushwood riverside tracks (the exquisite carved wooden *Dagenham Idol* from 2400 BC was found here), the medieval field system and the rusting ruins of military infrastructure — all combined together in a subtle open air theatre of memory.

Many pioneering exercises in ecological recovery are now happening in these backlands, once the capital's dumping ground. As London grew, a place was needed in which to locate its noxious industries and ungainly public utilities, as well as somewhere to dispose of its waste, and hide the victims of the city's poverty and social disruption. Gasworks, power stations, sewage farms, fever hospitals, asylums, landfill sites, hospital ships and prisons were all located downstream, and the city's polluted air was carried even further eastwards by the prevailing winds. Barges full of disinterred human bones from the city's reclaimed churchyards dumped their loads into the river near Tilbury. Meanwhile, life in the upper reaches of the Thames was promoted as wholesome, arcadian and good. We have been throwing things away for centuries, only recently realising that there is no such place as away. We all live downriver now.

Sources and further reading

Appleton, Jay, *The Symbolism of Habitat*, University of Washington Press, London, 1990

Baker, J. A., *The Peregrine, The Hill of Summer & Diaries*, Harper Collins, London, 2010

Baring-Gould, S., *Mehalah: A Story of the Salt Marshes*, The Boydell Press, Woodbridge, 1983

Bille, M., Hastrup, F., & Sorensen, T. F., *An Anthropology of Absence: Materializations of Transcendence and Loss*, Springer, London, 2010

Bonnefoy, Yves, *The Arrière-pays*, Seagull Books, Calcutta, 2012

Braudel, Fernand, *On History*, Weidenfeld & Nicolson, London, 1980

Collins, Ian, *James Dodds: Tide Lines*, Studio Fine Art Publications & Jardine Press, London, 2011

Constant, Caroline, *The Modern Architectural Landscape*, University of Minnesota Press, Minneapolis, 2012

Corbin, Alain, *The Lure of the Sea*, Penguin Books, London, 1995

Corke, David, *The Nature of Essex*, Barracuda Books, Buckingham, 1984

Cosgrove, Denis, *Social Function and Symbolic Landscape*, Barnes & Noble, New Jersey, 1985

Coveney, Michael, *Ken Campbell: The Great Caper*, Nick Hern Books, London, 2011

Countryside Agency, *Agricultural Landscapes: 33 Years of Change*, Wetherby, West Yorkshire, 2006

Clark, Kenneth, *Landscape into Art*, John Murray, London, 1976

Cunliffe, Barry, *Facing the Ocean: The Atlantic and its Peoples*, Oxford University Press, Oxford, 2001

Darley, Gillian, *Villages of Vision: A Study of Strange Utopias*, Five Leaves Publications, Nottingham, 2007

Doherty, Willie, *Disturbance*, Dublin City Gallery, Dublin, 2011

Edensor, Tim, *National Identity, Popular Culture and Everyday Life*, Berg, Oxford, 2002

English Heritage, *Twentieth-Century Military Sites: Current Approaches to their Recording and Conservation*, London, 2003

Evans, Gareth & Robson, Di (editors), *Towards Re-Enchantment: Place and Its Meanings*, Art Events, London, 2010

Everitt, Eileen, *The Development of Lower Mayland and Maylandsea During the 20th Century*, Maylandsea, 2007

Fairbrother, Nan, *New Lives, New Landscapes*, Penguin Books, Harmondsworth, 1972

Farley, Paul & Roberts, Michael Symmons, *Edgelands: Journeys into England's True Wilderness*, Jonathan Cape, London, 2011

Fautley, Matthew & Garon, James, *The Essex Coastline — Then and Now*, Potton Publishing, South Gloucestershire, 2004

Flam, Jack (editor), *The Collected Writings of Robert Smithson*, University of California Press, London, 1996

Ford, Laura Oldfield, *Savage Messiah*, Verso, London, 2011

Gilbert, Bob, 'Of spectacle and species' in *London 2012: How Was it for Us?*, Mark Perryman (editor), Lawrence & Wishart, London, 2013.

Gillingham, D. W., *Unto The Fields*, illustrated by Harry A. Pettit, The Country Book Club, London, 1955

Green, L. S. (editor), *The Essex Landscape: In Search of its History*, Essex County Council, Chelmsford, 1999

Grieve, Hilda, *The Great Tide: The Story of the 1953 Flood Disaster in Essex*, Essex Record Office, Chelmsford, 1959

Groom, Nick, 'The people betrayed by the lie of the land' in *The Independent*, London, 10 December 2010

Hardy, Dennis, *Utopian England: Community Experiments 1900–1945*, E. & F. N. Spon, London, 2000

Hardy, Dennis & Ward, Colin, *Arcadia for All: The Legacy of a Makeshift Landscape*, Five Leaves, Nottingham, 2004

Harman, Claire, *Sylvia Townsend Warner: A Biography*, Minerva, London, 1991

Harris, Alexandra, *Romantic Moderns: English Writers, Artists and the Imagination from Virginia Woolf to John Piper*, Thames & Hudson, London, 2010

Hoskins, W. G., *The Making of the English Landscape*, Book Club Associates, London, 1977

Howkins, Alun, 'The Discovery of Rural England' in *Englishness: Politics and Culture 1880–1920*, Colls, Robert & Dodd, Philip (editors), Croom Helm, London, 1986

Ingold, Tim, *The Perception of the Environment: Essays on Livelihood, Dwelling and Skill*, Routledge, London, 2000

Lewis, Jim, *Industry and Innovation: The Technological Revolution in the Lea Valley*, Libri Publishing, Oxfordshire, 2010

Jarman, Derek, *Modern Nature*, Vintage, London, 1991

Keiller, Patrick, *The Possibility of Life's Survival on the Planet*, Tate Publishing, London, 2012

Mabey, Richard, *The Unofficial Countryside*, Sphere Books, London, 1978

Mabey, Richard, *Weeds: The Story of Outlaw Plants*, Profile Books, London, 2012

Mack, John, *The Sea: A Cultural History*, Reaktion Books, London, 2011

Matless, David, *Landscape and Englishness*, Reaktion Books, London, 1998

Macfarlane, Robert, 'Walk the line' in *The Guardian*, London, 23 May 2009

Macfarlane, Robert, *The Old Ways*, Hamish Hamilton, London, 2012

McInnes, Robin & Stubbings, Hope, *Art as a Tool in Support of the Understanding of Coastal Change in East Anglia*, Crown Estate, London, 2010

Meyer, Morgan, 'Placing and tracing absence: a material culture of the immaterial' in *Journal of Material Culture* 17 (1) 103–110, 2012

Monbiot, George, *Feral: Searching for Enchantment on the Frontiers of Rewilding*, Allen Lane, London, 2013

Murry, John Middleton, *Community Farm*, Peter Nevill Ltd, London, 1952

Natural England, *Coastal Access*, Peterborough, 2010

Norberg-Schulz, Christian, *The Concept of Dwelling*, Electra/Rizzoli, New York, 1985

Pretty, Jules, *This Luminous Coast*, Full Circle Editions, Woodbridge, Suffolk, 2011

Rackham, Oliver, *The History of the Countryside*, Phoenix, London, 2004

Ray, Andrew, 'Far in the wild His steps were driven' at http://some-landscapes.blogspot.co.uk, 2012

Robinson, Tim, *Connemara: Listening to the Wind*, Penguin, London, 2006

Rodwell, John, 'Forgetting the land', Reckitt lecture text, M. B. Reckitt Trust, Hitchin, Hertfordshire, 2006

Salisbury, Martin (editor), *Artists at the Fry*, Ruskin Press, Cambridge, 2003

Saunders, Gill (editor), *Recording Britain*, V&A Publishing, London, 2011

Schalansky, Judith, *Atlas of Remote Islands*, Penguin, London, 2010

Schama, Simon, *Landscape and Memory*, Harper Collins, London, 1995

Scruton, Roger, *News from Somewhere*, Continuum, London, 2004

Sebald, W. G., *Austerlitz*, Penguin Books, London, 2002

Sinclair, Iain, *Edge of the Orison*, Hamish Hamilton, London, 2005

Soper, Kate, *What is Nature?*, Blackwell, Oxford, 2001

Spalding, Frances, *Prunella Clough: Regions Unmapped*, Lund Humphries, Farnham, 2012

Tolhurst, Peter, *East Anglia: A Literary Pilgrimage*, Black Dog Books, Bungay, Suffolk, 1996

Treib, Marc (editor), *Representing Landscape Architecture*, Taylor & Francis, Oxon, 2008

Tufnell, Ben, *Land Art*, Tate Publishing, London, 2006

Virilio, Paul, *Bunker Archeology*, Les Éditions Du Semi-Cercle, Paris, 1994

Walser, Robert, *The Walk*, Serpent's Tail, London, 1992

Walsham, Alexandra, *The Reformation of the Landscape*, Oxford University Press, 2011

Ward, Colin, 'A century of land settlement in Essex' in *Talking Green*, Five Leaves, Nottingham, 2012

Warner, Sylvia Townsend, *The True Heart*, Virago, London, 1981

Warner, Sylvia Townsend, 'The Essex Marshes' in *With the Hunted: Selected Writings*, Black Dog Books, Norwich, 2012

Williams, Raymond, *The Country and the City*, Chatto & Windus, London, 1973

Woodward, Christopher, *In Ruins*, Chatto & Windus, London, 2001

Worpole, Ken, *Last Landscapes: The Architecture of the Cemetery in the West*, Reaktion Books, London, 2003

Worpole, Ken & Orton, Jason, *350 Miles: An Essex Journey*, Essex County Council, Chelmsford, 2005

Wright, Patrick, *The Village that Died for England*, Jonathan Cape, London, 1995

Wright, Patrick, *The River: The Thames in Our Time*, BBC, London, 1999

Yearsley, Ian, *Islands of Essex*, Ian Henry Publications, Romford, 2000

Key to the photographs

Acknowledgements

This essay was based on various talks and writings on the contemporary English landscape undertaken since the publication of *350 Miles: An Essex Journey* in 2005. As a result of that book I began a correspondence with a number of people on issues of shared concern. Some of these exchanges led to invitations to speak at seminars and conferences and in other ways share ideas on the challenging nature of 21st century landscape æsthetics.

I am grateful to Robert Macfarlane and Marina Warner, both centrally involved in two seminal conferences at the Centre for Research in the Arts, Social Sciences and Humanities (CRASSH) at Cambridge University: 'Passionate Natures: Ecology and the Imagination' (2007) and 'Memory Maps: Image, Place and Story' (2008) and to Jules Pretty at Essex University for many things, including the invitation to give the prestigious 2011 Burrows Lecture, part of which was woven into this essay. Tom Conroy of DP World London Gateway and Joe and Vicky Backhouse kindly provided access to coastal sites normally unavailable, and deserve special thanks.

Thanks are also due to Gareth Evans, writer and curator, who edited the seminal collection of poems, essays and images, *Towards Re-enchantment: Place and its Meanings*, in 2009, and who has subsequently brought together a number of sympathetic people exploring contemporary ecology and landscape in a series of annual weekend gatherings around the theme of 'Place' at the Snape Maltings in Suffolk. Gareth also provided meticulous editorial advice.

My meeting with photographer Jason Orton in 2004 — and our subsequent collaboration on *350 Miles* and other projects — has proved especially rewarding, as have many joint walks and expeditions in Essex, often joined by writer Gillian Darley. As always, the companionship and lifelong love of the Essex shoreline shared with my wife, photographer Larraine Worpole, remains enduring.

Finally I am grateful to the Leverhulme Trust for the award of an Emeritus Fellowship Grant towards the costs of preparing this book, and to colleagues at the Cities Institute, London Metropolitan University, for their continued interest and support.

— *Ken Worpole*

Colophon

The New English Landscape
Published by Field Station | London, in 2013

Photographs copyright © Jason Orton 2013
Text copyright © Ken Worpole 2013

This book was designed, typeset and made into pages in Adobe InDesign by Peter Brawne, Matter, London. The text was set in the typeface FF Quadraat Pro (designed by Fred Smeijers, Antwerp). The photographs were printed as C-types by Rob Sara. These were scanned, colour corrected and CMYK proofed by Touch Digital, London. The book was printed in Belgium by Cassochrome and bound in the Netherlands by Binderij Hexspoor, Boxtel

ISBN 978-0-9926669-0-3

A blog associated with this book can be found at:
www.thenewenglishlandscape.wordpress.com

Jason Orton: www.jasonorton.com
Ken Worpole: www.worpole.net